TURNING POINT
–
THE FALL & RISE

by
Yves Veulliet
(translation: Maxine Harfield-Neyrand)

TURNING POINT
—
THE FALL & RISE

Preface by Professor Claude Hamonet

originally published in French
by
L'Harmattan

© L'Harmattan, 2010
5-7, rue de l'Ecole-Polytechnique, 75005 Paris

Thanks to

Professor Claude Hamonet who resoundingly proves that intelligence of the heart lies at the heart of intelligence.

Isabelle Henkens, at the origin of this project, for her powerfully contagious enthusiasm!

Contents

Preface	1
1. Warning: Bend up ahead	9
2. The Croque-Monsieur effect or torture apparatus	13
3. Lessons in things	19
4. Traveling without moving	21
5. Towards challenges: the real world	25
6. Challenge or depression: home sweet home.... ?	29
7. Hit the road Jack!	31
8. A question of choice: great, so now what?	37
9. Choosing reintegration: heigh ho, heigh ho, it's off to work we go...	43
10: Reintegration means choices: a room with a view	49
11. Instructions for reintegration: let's get to work!	53
12. Reintegration continues in a straight line: the theory of perpetual movement	63
13. A turning point in reintegration: one man, two worlds	71
14. The gentle slope of reintegration: a mobile job with reduced mobility	77
15. A conclusion and two necessities: accessibility and…	79
First necessity: Access for people with disabilities: no. Access for everybody: yes!	81
Second necessity: Don't tell me you haven't thought about it?	85
Annex: How I have made my life bearable	89

Preface

Yves Veulliet's tale is quite remarkable. As someone familiar with the reeducation and fight against exclusion of people with disability, having experienced a number of similar stories at close hand, I have marveled at and been moved in my reading of such a realistic and positive account.

This is not the first book to treat the subject of *going under suddenly* or *taking a nose dive* (Marc Maury *Le plongeon… vers la vie,* 2002) or of the *sharp bend in the road* which, in a fraction of a second, forces you to discover that the world around you is, in fact, littered with obstacles which reflect your abnormality back at you, when it is in fact this actual world, our world to be precise, that is not *normal.* Our world has been conceived for a very particular type of adult human biped, not too short, not too tall or too fat, capable of rapidly seeing, hearing, reasoning, expressing him or herself when confronted by a whole network of natural or man-made obstacles: stairs, pavements, narrow passages, overly heavy doors, indecipherable signposts, ill-explained routes...

Yves Veulliet helps us to relive his initiatory journey into the world of disability and his triumph over it to gain a new type of freedom, by patiently accompanying us and sagely understanding our surprise and ignorance at his reality, in a manner I've never previously come across in similar works. The story of his journey from the accident to real life, very powerfully awakens in me, the image of my very

Turning Point

close friend, Gérard, also a paraplegic and enamoured of freedom, who used humour and self-derision in a similar style to that of Yves Veulliet.

The book is easy to read, because it is very well written in evocative language, often funny, sometimes raw, a little like Céline, always tender, expressing the author's enormous reserve of love. He knows how to get us to share with him his daily existence as a "paraplegic" person (to use the stigmatizing medical term), by dressing up his emotions in occasionally provocative, but never misplaced, words.

The episode with the anti-bedsore Stryker bed, which he calls "Croque-Monsieur" is a good example of a very 'ortho-paedic' therapeutic rigour which predominated at a certain time, as much in the area of skin complications as with organic problems (bedsores, kidney pain) which were dreaded by doctors who wrote, up until the 1950s, that survival with paraplegia seemed unthinkable to them. All of that has changed enormously and quasi-ritualistic practices have been 'humanised', but the question remains: beyond mere survival, how does one live with paraplegia in a world which is not, in theory, made for it? This is where Yves Veulliet asks all the real questions, with not inconsiderable talent.

First of all, at the care level, you have the attitude of health professionals. Although all trained in the illness, they have not yet been adapted to the disability itself or to its re-adaptation (in the real world), and that is true even of those who have chosen to make it their specialism. The majority among them continue to reason in terms of deficiencies, which calls to mind the degrading archaism of infirmity. The explicit negativity of language frequently beginning with "in" or "de" remains too common in rehabilitation

Preface

centres. Doctors, in particular, have not yet adapted their language to the new reality which is one of valorization, emphasising the positivity of a person's exisiting capacities despite their handicap due to an illness or traumatism injuring their body and turning their subjectivity upside down, that's to say, their self-perception, their environment, other people and the meaning of life.

This is very well expressed in the analysis of the word re-education which Yves Veulliet insists upon, following the example of my friend Professor Andrej Seyfried from Warsaw, former specialist at the World Health Organisation with whom I've shared a great deal professionally. Things are evolving though because, in our scientific meetings on rehabilitation medicine, we frequently speak of *therapeutic education*. The residual word *therapeutic* being, of course, too much on its own.

The transformation from illness to disability amongst doctor-rehabilitators has not yet happened. The rehabilitation service or the re-adaptation centre are transitory places visited between the illness and disability stages. You enter them as an ill or injured person and leave with disabilities for life. The interior journey into disability which Yves Veulliet invites us to take with him, is not dissimilar to the one Robert Murphy provides for us: this American anthropologist who also became paraplegic then tetraplegic (paralysed in all four limbs), wrote *The Body Silent* (1987), translated into French as *Vivre à corps perdu* (1992). Yves Veulliet describes the body's silence so well, when his doesn't respond to orders to move, or fails to transfer the feeling of the physiotherapist's hands as he/she tries to mobilise his legs. The *lost body* must be replaced by another way of being 'whole', as stated by the fantastical tribune, influential cousin of the King of

Turning Point

Morocco and doctor who declared vehemently in 1992, showing his empty eye socket to a room filled with people with disabilities, at the Fair exhibition in Casablanca at a conference organised by the Amical Association of Moroccan Handicapped People: "You are whole Men, I am missing one eye but I am whole, you are whole, we are all human". Throughout his story, Yves Veulliet explains to us how he too, once again, became a *whole man.*

Above and beyond the already complex but surmountable problems of daily existence with a paraplegic body, Yves Veulliet sends us two crucial messages on what are, still today, the two main obstacles which impact people with disabilities and particularly, but not exclusively, people with medullary injuries: accessibility and sexuality. Two taboo subjects in societies in the grip of 'architectural and urbanistic order' and 'sexual order'. We need to invest in these two bastions in order to bring to the word autonomy its true meaning of liberation.

The best thing is to quote Yves Veulliet whose two attacks have our strong approval. The cautiousness of mayors, directors of public or private establishments, tradesmen etc is absolutely revolting and should be vigorously denounced as long as the prejudice suffered by victims of these ridiculously conformist and archaic attitudes is at large.

> *I know that like me you go to the cinema, the theatre, for a drink, or even, let's be crazy!, to the post office or the town hall. If you have to climb up three steps or a narrow doorway to access a building, you have no difficulty but for me and the millions of people like me, it causes a whole load of frustration, imposed*

Preface

> *inequalities and stupid material limitations which often have a naughty habit of wiping the beatific smile from my face, time and time again! Whether you are involved in public office, a tradesman... Accessibility is not a question of handicap, it concerns us all! Go on, pass it on!*

The dead end on sexuality and its real aspects is only too common. Reeducation centres are perceived as being asexualised as Robert Murphy already observed when mentioning that he was hopsitalised in a bedroom in which the doctors had failed to notice that there was a woman. It's he as well who expresses with regret that the doctors who re-educated him and took care of him so well with respect to his autonomy in using the wheelchair and carrying out toilet functions never asked him the question: "How does it feel to be a tetraplegic?"

Sexuality being excluded from conversations. However, it holds an essential place in the life of a woman and a man as Teilhard de Chardin wrote so well:

> *Love is the most universal, the most formidable of cosmic energies... socially we feign ignore it in science, in business, in meetings, although, surreptitiously, it's everywhere. Immense, ubiquitous and always insubordinate, it seems we will finish by never fully understanding or capturing this savage force... (L'Amour 1997)*

In Yves Veulliet's own words:

> *"Could I still be attractive to women?" And its corollary: If so, how do you make love without*

Turning Point

moving your legs? And the sensation, would I still feel something? And the woman, would it turn her on or would she struggle to stifle a yawn?

These were questions of the utmost importance, but who could I ask? If I have a problem concerning my blood circulation, there's no cultural pressure to prevent me from questioning the doctors about it, but on the subject of slap and tickle, it was another case entirely. The doctors who came to see me in my room during their rounds asked me: "So how's it going today? Ready for your physio? You should be eating a bit more!" No male or female doctor for that matter ever turned up to ask the following questions: "So, still waking up with an erection? And pulling birds in the corridors, that going okay? How many women's heads have you turned today?"

One or two doctors at the rehabilitation centre were able to answer my questions on the quality of erection and ejaculation and on my chances of having children, that's to say from a scientific, technical point of view.

…when they teach us to climb kerbs in our chair, there is a physio with us; when we practice putting our wheelchair in the car, there is an occupational therapist with us; when we have to relearn how to make love, who's there to help? Who guides us? Who educates us? The response is blindingly clear: nobody, Jack shit, nothing, not a chance!

So, at the risk of setting teeth gnashing among the respectable classes or narrow-minded doctors: in the same way that there are nurses, occupational therapists,

Preface

> *doctors, physios, social workers and others who are there to help and guide us in our new lives, why not automatically include sexual reeducation as part of the standard programme?... Yes it's trivial, yes it's shocking, yes it's inconvenient..."*

No it's not, we say, it's not shocking, it's the honest reality of being human and should be respected.

Yves Veulliet's vigorous words help us to better understand the gulf that exists between people with disabilities and those who '*treat*' them. This is where Yves Veulliet's personal account has the most value for everyone: people concerned by the same problems as him, professionals and students, future professionals of rehabilitation who should all read this book before embarking on this specialism or continuing to practice it, but also, shopkeepers and those in positions of responsibility who we've elected for more kinship but also for equality and, and even more so, for freedom without which Man is not Man.

Professor Claude Hamonet
*Specialist in Physical Medicine and Rehabilitation
Doctor of Social Anthropology, Ex-Handicap and
Rehabilitation Specialist for the World Health Organisation
Ex-Director of UFR Communication and
Reinsertion in Society (University Paris 12)
Specialist (rehabilitation medicine) recognised by the Cour de Cassation,
Doctor at l'Hôtel-Dieu, Paris*

Turning Point

1. Warning: Bend up ahead

I should have accepted. I should have gone to eat at my mate's house like he suggested after watching him play tennis. But no, "I'm going home" I said. I started up my 250cc bike, there was sun and blue sky and a quiet tree-lined road, the cushy life.

Well nearly...some gravel on a sharp bend, the back wheel skids, the bend turns into a straight line with a pretty violent landing in a ditch four metres below. Black hole. Curtains.

They informed me later that my motorcycle hadn't come off too badly, just the fork and handlebars buckled. Me, well I was a little less fortunate than the bike, as I discovered when I woke up in hospital. There was a bloke in white at the foot of my bed who seemed quite friendly, and to my left, I could make out a nurse, hidden behind a whole load of pipes attached to my nose, my arm and in particular, a large tube in my chest. I wasn't in pain, morphine is amazing, you float along...gently.

I came back down to earth with a bump when I heard the gentleman at the end of my bed say: "I'm the surgeon who just operated on your spine, you've got two broken vertebrae and your spinal cord has been damaged. It's too early to say any more. Get some rest".

Turning Point

Ah great so my spinal cord has been damaged. I thought back to my biology lessons at 15 or 16 years old when I'd learned about the role of the spinal cord in providing the crucial link between the brain and the rest of the body. I would never have imagined the extent to which I was going to be painfully reminded of this for the rest of my life...

It was 12th July 1987, precisely 21 years and 7 days since my parents' misty-eyed and bedazzled gaze fell for the first time upon their little bawling, fidgeting marvel who would grow up to be a strapping fellow over 6 foot tall, standing upright on his own two feet and ready to devour life, as they say in the self-help books that are all the rage. In fact, standing, from here on in was going to be a darn sight harder to achieve, but at that precise moment, in that hospital bedroom, it still seemed completely normal to me to be able to stand. Yeah, that was it, it didn't seem easy or difficult, just normal.

After a few days, they started to take off the tubes, all of them, bit by bit. It hurt my back a little but I started to sit up, as it was more pleasant to be able to eat by myself without having to being fed: I'd never fantasised about being a little bird. And so the days went by with visits from family and friends. My Mum, always there, from the start of the visits to the last. Her eyes were red, very red, but it's only now in writing these lines, that this memory comes back to me. For her sake, I wish I'd remembered earlier. My Dad never came to see me. He had an excellent excuse: he had died from an aortic aneurism the previous year.

Five times a week, the physio comes in the morning to move my legs. It's weird, but I don't feel his hands on my legs, they just tingle a bit inside like when you sleep too long on a squashed hand. When I try to move them,

1. Warning: Bend up ahead

nothing happens but I'm not worried. According to the doctors, my spinal cord and my body are in what they call "medullary shock". It can take up to three months before the body comes alive again.

The grounds I could see from my window were pretty, a series of well-kept, even flowerbeds in bloom, with a few trees here and there. And on certain days, when the window was open, and this was often the case: it can get hot, even in Belgium, stifling at times in summer, the nice smell of the freshly cut grass wafted in. And for the month, almost, that I'd been stuck in that bedroom, I had had ample time to look at it, the garden. For a moment there, I thought I'd become a fan of gardening... no, don't worry, I'm only kidding! This was when they came to announce some extraordinary news to me: the very next day, they were going to transfer me to a rehabilitation centre in Brussels. Did you get that? A RE-HA-BIL-I-TA-TION centre, I was going to pull myself up on parallel bars on a black rubber mat surrounded by guys and girls in white coats encouraging me to retake my first steps. We'd have to see, I knew I would sweat like a pig to begin with but that didn't matter. If the price to pay for walking again was to have sweat rings under my arms and use nine sticks of deodorant per day, so be it, Amen!

Turning Point

2. The Croque-Monsieur effect or torture apparatus

The rehabilitation centre in Brussels was a bit on the old-fashioned side. Officially called the Centre for Traumatology & Rehabilitation, we called it CTR for short. As soon as I arrived, they transferred me from the ambulance stretcher onto a sort of thin, narrow mattress attached to a board on four wheels, surrounded by a type of steel frame. A bizarre machine, not uncomfortable but offering barely no margin for movement. The doctor there to meet me, a lot less friendly than the surgeon from the other hospital, explained to me that I would stay on the Stryker, the name of this thing, until I was able to sit in a wheelchair. At that point in time, I would be able to return to a normal bed. A wheelchair... why not, if it enabled me to get off this board as quickly as possible. The walls of my new room were pink in colour and must have been really pretty when first wallpapered, about 300 years ago... anyway, at least there was a TV.

I'd been alone there for two or three hours when two nurses who were jollier than they were pretty, came in with another plank in their hands, the same size as the one I was resting on and it was then that I understood the purpose of the steel frame surrounding me, me and my board mattress. Have you ever made a croque-monsieur? When one side is cooked, you close the top of the toaster, turn it over and the other side cooks. Are you with me? Good, so now imagine that I'm the croque-monsieur: I am lying on my

Turning Point

back and the two nurses attach their board to my forehead, my chest, my legs with the help of two big bolts on each side of the metal frame and, here we go! , they turn the whole thing over and I end up on my stomach. They then remove the board on which my back was resting and I'm there watching the floor with my back and my butt in the air! And there you have it for the next three hours in that position. The kind ladies in white explained to me that in order to avoid wounds and bedsores on my back, buttocks and heels caused by lack of movement, caused in turn my blood vessels being compressed for an abnormally long time, my position had to be changed every three hours. You can imagine my joy? I played front and back, back and front every three hours, day *and* night, for more than a month until I could get back to a normal bed.

There was another bed in the room, I mean a real bed, surrounded by a whole load of oriental decorations, but its occupant was not there when I arrived. They'd just turned me over onto my back again when I was introduced to my room mate. He'd just come into the room, his electric chair making the sound of an asthmatic hoover. "Hello" he said, he was an air pilot in the Pakistani army, he was a tetraplegic. I think I'm right in saying that I never knew exactly what happened to him, he only spoke English or Pakistani. We spent two months together, I could get by a little in Shakespeare's language, he spent his spare time watching cricket matches on TV. He wanted to teach me the rules, I pretended to understand.

After a month bathed in Pakistani music and smart gentleman dressed all in white, playing games on the small screen for hours with a ball and some stick ends, I was transferred to a room with four beds in which there were two other occupants.

2. The Croque-Monsieur effect or torture apparatus

Later, I would often pay a visit to my Pakistani friend, nobody had replaced me in the room. Fate is funny, without my accident, without this stay at the centre, I am certain I would never have passed so much time with someone so different from me, so removed from my culture, from my way of life. That's one of the reasons why I love life, for these scarcely imaginable meetings, for the shortcuts we take, or not. Enough of that,... I didn't go as far as subscribing to *Wisden* cricket magazine.

My two new room-mates had both been victims of car accidents. Rudy had had his spinal cord damaged at lower back level whilst Didier had been struck at neck level. All three of us were aged between 20 and 30, we came from the same social background, more or less, so the atmosphere was friendly.

Inevitably, we spoke about the lives we'd led 'before': Didier was crazy about rally cars and never missed an opportunity to tell us an anecdote on the subject. As for Rudy, also a car fan, it was always with a smile that he recalled his memories of being a student or on military service. Of the three of us, I think it was Didier, the oldest injured person in our room who was the first to take on board the fact that, as a tetraplegic, his life had irredeemably changed, he seemed calm about it. But as for Rudy and me, it was out of the question to regard ourselves as paraplegics! Stuck forever on this blasted croque-monsieur apparatus, our desire to put up a fight with our own bodies for us long as they let us, raged within us.

We spent many months together in the same room. If we'd got to know each other in more conventional circumstances, I don't think we would have been as close as we were at that time, but our shared horror at seeing

Turning Point

part of our bodies no longer obeying us created a real solidarity which did not waver the whole time we were hospitalised together.

Didier had already been in a proper bed for quite a long time, Rudy and I also dreamed of being once again able to return to a traditional bed. And then one morning, the nurses brought in a bed, a real one with a mattress, a pillow, the works, you know, a bed! It was for Rudy.

For us, to transfer to a proper bed, meant something, one step further towards real rehabilitation, we knew that after the bed, the next step would be a wheelchair and then, who knows, no more wheelchair! We wished for this so strongly that no doctor, nurse, voodoo sorcerer or god could have made us believe the contrary (even if it's true that the doctors never painted a glowing picture of any of this or about anything). We were going to kill ourselves, that we knew, but by god, in the end we'd get there and put one foot in front of the other! And as it turned out, it would be Rudy who was the first to throw himself into battle. Me, I watched him transfer to a bed from my front row seat, my mattress-board. I tried really hard to hide my jealousy, I don't think I succeeded.

Then it was my turn and I received my bed three weeks after Rudy. After the bed came the wheelchair, the machine in which I'd do my first wheel spins, expecting to improve of course. And what a magnificent model it was, this wheelchair must have been the recipient of about the same number of arses as there are stars in the Milky Way judging by the tired blue of the fabric and the faded chrome of the frame. After a few warm up exercises in bed, the physio and a nurse helped me to sit in my tank. I got back a bit of mobility, that's to say, I could leave

2. The Croque-Monsieur effect or torture apparatus

the bedroom, take a look at the corridors, the exercise rooms, the bar. But first of all I had to learn how to manoeuvre the chair, to make it turn when I wanted and, most importantly, in the direction I wanted. Have you ever carried a cumbersome object in your arms, and had the feeling that the space around you has suddenly become smaller given you are bumping into everything? Well, that's what learning to steer a wheelchair is like: starting from a narrow space though big enough for two legs, your new field of vision has to take into account four wheels and the surrounding frame. And that's just for everything on the horizontal. As for the vertical, given I was six foot and a few inches when standing, I was used to watching other people from above, now, sitting on my august posterior, I was in danger of , straining my neck from trying to look people in the eyes as we spoke. Oh well, I soon found out that being at bum level behind certain people wasn't wholly disadvantageous…

So, having bumped into almost all the furniture in my bedroom and scratched every side of the bed and bedside table like a feline marking out its territory, I got a surprise! On the way back from one of my U-turns, I was suddenly confronted with someone who looked familiar. He had greasy, thinning hair, he was badly shaven and as thin as he was pale. It was the mirror above the sink reflecting this image back to me, so this guy had to be me, this ghost. I couldn't believe it, it wasn't even funny, after serious internal haemorrhaging as a result of the accident, a few weeks without fresh air, hardly ever moving and constantly lying down and there you had it, the new Yves Veulliet had arrived, the shadow of the shadow of the shadow of his former self, the one from before 12th July.

Turning Point

In the end, I didn't go wandering the corridors that day, I didn't check out the exercise rooms or the bar, I didn't even try to break the mirror. I just asked the nurses to help me back to bed.

3. Lessons in things

Another morning, another nothing morning, sang Jean-Jacques Goldman – if only we could make it untrue. The nurse brought me my clothes and helped me slip them on before I got back into the wheelchair and tried to give myself a facelift with a good shampoo and electric shave, in an attempt to forget my ghostly appearance from the day before and prove to that cursed mirror that it had been wrong to show me that swine. My first breakfast in the refectory with the 'others', a big room with large windows on the right which let in light and reminded us that the outside still existed. The clink of spoons in bowls, the screeching of wheelchair tyres on linoleum, the forced (to a greater or lesser degree) laughter of 50, or perhaps 100 beings who were a lot luckier than me or even, a lot less, paraplegics, tetraplegics, amputees, or those bloody lucky devils who had nothing but a plaster cast (rare though they were!) So that was the refectory: noise, light and people whose faces reflected your own sorry state of affairs, without even meaning to.

It was a game, a game we all had to play, whether we wanted to or not. We had to be moving forward, whatever.

Learning to dress ourselves (try putting jeans on without standing up, you're going to have a laugh!), taking a pee sitting down without getting it everywhere, sitting on a toilet but not knowing how to get up again, opening a door when the front wheels of the chair get in your way... yet, as

Turning Point

a result of practising, willing, swearing, weeping, elbowing the walls, laughing desperately, you get there eventually: doors open, trousers slip off, bottoms stay dry, toilets are no longer a place of torture, just another obligatory step.

4. Traveling without moving

Before venturing further with my story, I must devote a few paragraphs to explain something essential to it, a phenomenon I noticed in myself and those surrounding me at the CTR. The next few lines in fact explain the rest of the book. Without these, dear Reader, the reason for the fundamental actions I take in the rest of the story would be obscured from you and you might regret having spent your money on buying this book rather than using it to purchase a DVD on aquaerobics among the Inuits of the Great North!

So my body started to find new bearings, in the end this was simply a question of mechanics: for each situation there was a corresponding movement which had to be carried out in the precisest way possible and eventually, the obstacle which seemed like an insurmountable mountain before our training sessions turned into a modest slope once we had mastered it. But that was the physical world, there was another world which didn't function along the same mechanical lines, a universe which bombarded our emotions with objective information at a rate that would make arthritic sluggards of our most powerful missiles. This internal world was different for each of us, yet was composed and ruled by the same basic element: our brain, 'the boss'. An organ of unimaginable complexity which, when we were faced with traumatic external events, imposed on us a succession of identical emotions which, however, differed in length of phase for each individual.

Turning Point

When a terrible event shatters our world, turns our life upside down, whether it wears the black mask of a loved one's death or the red of our murdered body, this event takes us on a path scattered with steps which are the same for everyone but which carry each of us along at different speeds. This path is not level: it starts with a painful descent, and when you've reached the bottom, you start to climb up and out along a gentler slope.

The first step leads you from shock to denial: starting with shock: "You have had an accident, your spinal cord is damaged", you move to denial: "It's true that I can no longer feel my legs, that I no longer have any control over them. But that won't last. I'm made of strong stuff, I'm strong willed, my body will get over it".

The second step ranges from denial to frustration and anger "Ah, well done Mother Nature, your protective mechanism is spot on, a simple jolt in the back and you lose 50% of your mobility. And they say it took you millions of years of evolution to come to such a crap conclusion! And what about those dickhead scientists who pump billions into playing games in space instead of dedicating them to making us walk again! And you over there, God, "rise up and walk", does that remind you of anything? Well, get to work!".

Frustration is followed by depression, passivity "Okay great, everything's fucked. Here I am, stuck in this shitpile of a wheelchair! That's it for girls, you can forget walks along the beach or in the forest, motorbikes: file them all away as memories." This is the hardest step, you hit rock bottom: everything is black, nothing has any taste anymore. Some people get stuck at this stage for months, years even. Sometimes they try to hide their latent despair

4. Traveling without moving

by ranting or with violence, too much alcohol or drugs. Those close to them suffer and turn away from them, which only accentuates their troubles.

The first three chapters which precede this one skim over these three steps. The journey does not take place along a linear path, depending on events, we might return to the previous step, just momentarily, before getting back on track, in the right direction.

Let's get back on track and leave these gloomy depths: little by little there is light and it grows bigger and bigger, it lights up the small piece of hope which makes us believe that life can still be worthwhile, even if only a little. We are drawn to the light, it makes us desirous once more to push beyond limits we thought were unsurpassable, we cast away our passivity to climb on to the next step, where challenges await, with the strength to climb higher kerbs, push through heavier doors or put on trousers worthy of the name (and not just those hideous, shapeless tracksuit bottoms worn simply out of resignation because they are easy to pull over the bum when seated).

And the uphill climb continues: after the challenges step, comes the choices step "I know I am continuing to progress and learn things which demonstrate that, even if my life today is clearly less pleasant than the one from 'before', it can still bring me moments of joy from time to time. In which case, what am I going to do with my life? Do my choices, my desires, correspond with something I can realistically achieve?"

And so finally, the last stage can be seen on the horizon, the one that will reunite us with a road from which fate brutally separated us, forcing us to take a battered path

Turning Point

through the fields, a path strewn with a crisscrossing of dead trees. I call this junction where we are forced to leave the tortured path to get back on the main road 'reintegration', the beginning of something which might not be too bad as long as we make the effort.

At the end of this slightly didactic but nevertheless essential chapter, let's return to the flow of this gripping tale which even Monsieur Fontaine wouldn't hesitate to steal from me as he did with Aesop, whose fables he made his *own*. So you can place me on the path that I've just described, the chapter titles which follow will begin with the name of each step at which I found myself.

5. Towards challenges: the real world

Time passed, individual or group exercises three times per week, plus physio sessions to get us back in good shape, enabling us to manoevre our chairs to a better and better degree, we even learned how to climb up and down kerbs, to ride on two wheels. Rudy annoyed me: he climbed up higher kerbs than me, he managed to ride on two wheels so easily he could even do it in reverse, whereas I had a hard enough just moving three metres forward. It was true that the level of his injury, the place where his spinal cord had been hit was lower than mine, so his balance was better for all that stuff, but that aside, it annoyed me all the same!

One October morning, as grey and humid as only a November morning could rival, Raymond, the physiotherapist responsible for our morning group exercises, put on a mocking expression to announce: "Today we are going on a walk outside the centre", there were four of us there that day, ready for our usual, morning reeducation session in the main gym hall. Although all different in colour, our eight eyes took on a look of puppy-eyed incredulity, as if Raymond had just pronounced the sentence "Okay lads, ready for a trip on a flying carpet?".

But our dilated pupils made no difference and we headed for the direction of the gates at the exit to the centre.

Turning Point

We were going to be confronted with real life for the first time, not the well-chartered life of the hospital and its grounds, but the one in which pavements are not straight, and kerbs are high, very high, too high, one in which the entrances to houses are five steps up, and in particular, one in which you have to face other people's stares, people like you or me from 'before', who are not used to seeing guys in wheelchairs pushing their machines by themselves, without even a tartan blanket to cover their knees, wearing tracksuit bottoms instead, in a colour which would make an adult chameleon feel sick. Their look pierces through you like an arrow of pity, of distaste even, its surgical precision aimed straight for the heart. All four of us made out as if we'd ignored these more or less discreet stares, but the effort was lost. It was easier to try to forget to breathe.

After two hours of this walk which was about as joyous as burying your favourite pet, we were happy to return to the rehabilitation centre, a bit like when you're given hot chocolate to drink because you are freezing inside. Just to crush us completely, Raymond thought it a good idea to add before we left "Great stuff lads, same again tomorrow if it's not raining" Non-Belgians think it rains a lot in Belgium, it was the first time I'd ever wished they were right…

The weeks passed, we were more and more at ease with our wheelchairs, both at the centre and outside. We were less and less frightened of pavements and kerbs that were a bit high, as for looks from other people… well, at least with the wheelchair things weren't going too badly.

Being able to manoeuve my wheelchair well was one thing, but I didn't want to leave it there, I wanted to WALK! But as far as my legs went, nothing, not the least sensation, not

5. Towards challenges: the real world

the least movement, it had been a few months now and still nothing. And what if they were really buggered? And what if all my willpower wasn't enough? And what if the last step for me was the chair and not walking again?

Rudy and me sometimes asked each other the same question to comfort each other with our mutual response, always the same: Of course we would walk again, just needed a bit of patience that was all...

Turning Point

6. Challenge or depression: home sweet home.... ?

Now that I could manage my wheelchair quite well, the time had come to learn how to leave it in order to get into a car, the bathtub, sit on a couch... in short, relearning how to do most of life's daily gestures.

I, like all the other paraplegics, was in a hurry to become completely autonomous, before walking again. Why were we in such a hurry? Well, because the rule at the rehabilitation centre was that if we were able to demonstrate a good level of autonomy, we could go home for the weekend and return to the centre on Sunday evening! I don't know who at the centre had come up with this idea, but he or she was one smart cookie, because I can assure you that there was no motivation like it. A horse never runs faster than when he smells his stables!

So there you have it, on a Saturday in November 1987 very early in the morning, one of my uncles came to collect me to take me home by car. It was cold, I didn't care, it was raining, I didn't care, there were idiots on the motorway, I couldn't have cared a less, I was going home, HOME.

To help you understand what I write further on, I need to explain something about the house where I grew up: it's a working-class house, sensibly stuck next to other dwellings in a long, almost uninterrupted line from the start of the road, without a garage and a single entrance reached after climbing up three steps, my bedroom was upstairs. Do you see where this is leading? Home was no longer entirely home: at home, I could come back alone (I often amused myself by jumping over the second entrance step), at home, I slept upstairs having scaled 18 stairs, at home, when I needed a book from high up on the bookshelf it was me who reached for it. So there you have it, after five months spent away from home, when I came back it was to get a punch in the face, even though I knew without wishing to admit it to myself, that here too, things would never be the same. I knew that soon the steps at the front door were going to be removed and replaced by a concrete ramp, I noticed that the living room had disappeared to make space for my bed (at least that hadn't changed!), that they'd added a toilet to the bathroom in addition to the original one which was inaccessible by wheelchair. I realised all the effort my mother, my family and my friends had gone to so that everything would be ready for my first night at the house, so I smiled and waited to be all alone in bed, I owed them that at least, before I cried my eyes out.

7. Hit the road Jack!

Week after week, back at the CTR, my physical aptitude improved, I could, for example, get in and out of a car by myself and fold and put the wheelchair inside on my own. Let's stay on this subject for a second: the car. You are perhaps unaware of this but you don't need legs to drive a car. I can just imagine your eyebrow raised in a '^' shape when reading that sentence, but just imagine, all you need to add is an axle to link the brake and acceleration pedals to the steering wheel and you're on! For the pernickety among you reading this, I should specify that it's easier to adapt an automatic car to this system but it's equally possible with a manual car, if you don't mind playing around with the gears. The only hitch is, when you've spent quite a lot of time driving with your feet, like most people and like me, even if they no longer work, you still think with them – not your hands – at the moment of braking or accelerating. I'll leave it to you to imagine the disastrous consequences of this state of affairs were they to let us out on our lovely roads, without further preparation. So the lawmakers, in their infinite wisdom, insist that new users of these manual drives who drove 'normal' cars before, must have lessons in a special vehicle and take a practical test. I used my time in rehabilitation to learn to drive a manual car with a specialist driving school, practising on the numerous park roads surrounding the CTR and after a few near misses with walls and stalling lamentably a good few times, I was able, little by little, to get used to this new style of driving and pass the test in

Turning Point

real traffic. For most people, having a car is synonymous with ease and flexibility in getting about. But for us, those who can no longer walk, being behind the wheel, is to regain access to a side of life we knew before, one that everyone can enjoy… and just for a moment, you almost get to like traffic jams, well almost… Besides, taking a bus, tram or underground train in a wheelchair more closely resembles an expedition to the Amazonian jungle in high heels and a Chanel suit than a healthy stroll. The level of accessibility to public transport and civic buildings in Belgium is so mediocre that on the rare occasions when I do find a ramp or a lift, I have trouble holding back a tear of incredulous joy.

But I digress, let's get back to the flow of this thrilling tale for which, any day now, Steven Spielberg will no doubt want to buy the rights. It seemed almost a bit weird to me when, in April 1988, the head doctor came to inform me that my time at the CTR was up, my reeducation was complete. I have always found the term 're-education' ridiculous, it should be called education: getting dressed sitting down, opening doors when seated, playing basket ball in a chair, stepping over curbs when seated, etc… I didn't *relearn* these things, but it is true that I would have preferred never to have had to learn them at all. I think it was at this moment that I accepted the fact that, as long as science had yet to find a way to even partially repair my spinal cord to allow me to walk again, I should look at life, my life, from the perspective of my four wheels and no longer on two feet. As I explained earlier, Rudy and I went through the same steps, but I think at that moment, his belief that he would walk again was stronger than mine.

I'm often asked how I accepted the fact that I would no longer walk, but I accepted nothing of the sort. It is

7. Hit the road Jack!

humanly impossible to accept the fact that at midday on 12th July 1987 I was walking like every other normally constituted person and that ten minutes and a shock to my back later, I would no longer be capable of it. Accepting such a thing would be like resigning from your own life, no, I simply assimilated the objective fact that, from thereon, my life would no longer be standing but sitting. How that would translate itself to my daily life, at that moment, by god, I had no idea...

The evening before I left, I celebrated my departure in my room with a few patients and some members of staff; I had a few nice beers kept aside which didn't last the night. But don't get any ideas about an evening of squalid bingeing, getting plastered and parapelgia don't go very well together: when you only have the top half of your body and your arms left to maintain a semblance of stability, if you add too many hops, fermented grape juice or any other liqueur made from malted grains to this delicate balance, you can expect your wheelchair to unilaterally declare its independence and find yourself in contact with a not very friendly floor you hadn't suspected would be so hard!

After the party night came the morning of saying goodbye to my roommates, the doctors, nurses, physios, occupational therapists, social workers...in brief, everyone I'd mixed with on an almost daily basis for the past eight months, practically the full-term of a pregnancy, and now I was leaving them all behind. All the male and female paraplegics, tetraplegics, amputees etc who like me have spent quite a lot of time at a rehabilitation centre will have a strange love-hate relationship with the place. The CTR effectively became witness to our failures, our hopes, our pain but also a stage on which to play out our small victories

Turning Point

over ourselves, the victories which led us to live more or less in peace with our new selves; different from the old one but not radically. We love this place but we hate this place. We are happy to have been able to experience things here which we would have liked to forget about forever.

It so happened that I saw Rudy and Didier again after we had all left the CTR. Inevitably, our relationship had changed since we'd been apart from each other. Although we had shared a good part of the road together, ultimately, each of us was following his own path.

We all have strategies for survival, a code we impose on ourselves in order to give a minimum of sense to our life, to make this thing we call life bearable: it may be music, amassing a fortune, believing in Self,... And so in my case, since I'd been born a second time, with a weaker hand than the first time round , my strategy was this: "onwards and upwards, straight ahead only". There is a box in my head, equipped with a big rusty lock, under which is written "Prior to 12th July 1987, definitively closed". Though sometimes, rarely, a few little flashes from the past resurface in the course of looking at a photo or hearing the sound of a motorbike engine, it's fine, on the whole, I keep that all safely locked away.

Despite this, the hardest thing when something happens to you that will have terrible consequences for the rest of your days, is that your reference points, the markers that helped you to manage your life as well as possible up until then, are turned upside down, unhinged; without having sought it, you leave a world you knew pretty well to plunge into an uncertain present and future which you already know are less pleasant and a lot more difficult than what you've experienced until that point. You set out in search

7. Hit the road Jack!

of the new possibilities and limits this future holds. A bit like a kid learning to walk who falls over ten times, twenty times, before, by force of trial and error, it manages to take a few steps. It was a bit like that for me too, I didn't have the choice, I had to move forward, differently from before but always forward. In fact, when I say I didn't have the choice, yes, we always have the choice; we can stop everything right here, now, take the great leap. Did I ever consider it? I'll leave you to guess...

Turning Point

8. A question of choice: great, so now what?

So there I was at home, the first weeks were quite pleasant, trying to find my bearings in my new environment. My mother was intelligent enough to put her maternal instincts aside and leave me to discover my own new way of doing things. There was no more mirror above the shelf in the bathroom, too high; had to add an extension to the table in the dining room otherwise my knees would no longer fit under it. One adjustment was horrendous, a nightmare even: the kitchen sink was inaccessible to me because of the piece of furniture it stood on, which I couldn't slide under, so, to my great despair, I was unable to do the washing up! My fellow gentlemen, you who are constantly looking for often very woolly excuses to avoid household chores, you have to admit that becoming paraplegic is hard to beat!

Little by little the weeks passed punctuated with bodybuilding sessions at home, I had kept some dumbbells from 'before' which I used to tone the muscles in my upper body to the maximum. When you only have two arms and two shoulders left to cover the movements usually made by your feet, legs, knees and hips, it's in your best interest to work on a solid top half! In addition to my personal little 'bodybuilding' routine, a physiotherapist came a few times a week to play with my legs, which made up a bit for their immobility and prevented the bones from becoming too fragile. Notwithstanding the physio, having now not walked for nearly a year, my thigh and calf muscles had

Turning Point

melted away and I found myself with legs long and slim enough to make the most anorexic of top models green with envy, including the hairs. Overall, weekends and the end of the week were the most fun. Family and friends came to down a glass or two with you, telling you about their jobs, the idiot referee who should never have whistled penalty, the latest film by Thingy in which Thingamabob should have refused to star, life, in short!

Speaking of family and friends, they can be fitted into two categories: the peeping toms, those who come to watch the 'casualty', who offer him a box of chocolates with an embarrassed smile and try to stimulate their feeble imagination by filling in the blanks in conversation with their ineptitudes. Of course, I take a perverse pleasure in not saying anything to fill the blanks, in order to maintain their uneasiness. Having suffered this torture for a length of time they deem socially acceptable, they get up, wishing me good luck and leave without forgetting to tell me of course that they will be back "as soon as possible" that's to say never, not really a great loss. And then there are the others, the good ones: those who come to see *you*, who take you for a ride in the car whilst I'm waiting to get mine, who make you laugh, who tell you interesting, relevant, shocking, moving things. Unfortunately, this second category of person is more rare...

Summer arrived, with sun and blue sky for company, your morale is always higher and the brain takes advantage to force you to ask yourself questions like "Now that you are starting to get used to yourself, what are you going to do at home other than watch the houseplants grow in the dining room?"

8. A question of choice: great, so now what?

So, should I work? Study? Mess around? Inclination or duty? The old Cornelian dilemma. As I have already said, I was condemned to move forward with my life. Sorry for the bad play on words but when you are paralysed, it's immobility that is the real enemy. Let's examine each choice carefully, beginning with the option "Do absolutely nothing": tempting, easy, not very lucrative with only my government allowance but I had no rent to pay and believe my mother would have torn out her eyes with her teeth if I'd proposed I contribute to household expenses with my allowance. Tempting, for sure, and no doubt, if I had been 50 at the time, I would have chosen this solution without hesitation... but as it was, I'd been 22 years old since 5th July 1988, and messed-up spinal cord or not, my neurons were screaming in my ears: "move, do, react, love, hate, live!" so doing zilch had to be binned. Second option: "studying". In 1988, no higher education establishment was really accessible for those with disabilities, I don't think things are radically different today either. There were always correspondance courses, yeah why not.... But no, I didn't want to do that, I was boiling up inside, I was frothing over, no, studying for two or four or more years, even by correspondence, no, that also seemed like inertia to me, stuck in one place, static. For me, survival meant movement, and as fast as possible.

When I contemplate my choices from the standpoint of someone now in his forties, I believe that the study path, exploring knowledge, would not have been too bad for me. I chose the third option, however, a job. Very well, excellent choice, motivating, exciting, captivating, fine but doing what? And where? My qualifications: secondary education to 18 and two out of three years of university studies in French and History were a bit light on my CV to go after an MD position with chauffeur, stock options and a golden parachute.

So, what should I do? Find a mundane but safe job in an office? Yeah, nah not very sexy. Telephone sales? "Hello, Mrs Boudard, good morning, this is Yves calling from Schmurtz company. Today is your lucky day, if you come and visit our showroom this Saturday, you will receive a hairdryer! Sorry? What was that? You've lost all your hair through chemo? That doesn't matter, you can always use it for drying your dog's hair!" No, definitely not my thing…in which case what was for heaven's sake??

And that's where the NFSRD came in. No, I'm not joking, it's not an acronym I've invented to make everyone feel more relaxed, like Never Feel Stupid Riding Dodos, I'm referring to the National Fund for the Social Redeployment of the Disabled. It's true we spend our time criticising those we're governed by (it has to be said in passing that we elect them too…) and often rightly so; this does not detract from the fact that thanks to a telephone call from this organisation on a fine sunny morning in August 1988, I was able to set out on a fascinating journey into the world of work "Mr Veulliet? Hello, the NFSRD on the line. A school in Brussels is looking for someone to take care of transferring their entire administration system to computer. It's a short-term, part-time contract with the possibility of being taken on full-time in the future. If you are interested, you should show up at 2pm next Wednesday. They'll be waiting for you".

Was I interested?! Of course it interested me, a part-time job plus a small additional disability allowance, that would be enough to live on okay on my own, not, no doubt, enough for me to buy a château on the banks of the Loire

8. A question of choice: great, so now what?

but hey... It so happened that at the CTR, after hours of physiotherapy and before the arrival of visitors, there were two or three hours to kill. Instead of staring at the little box of moving pictures and the news reported by hacks who, incidentally, assume the air of bailiffs when announcing the latest air disaster but whose look lights up briefly at the moment they say "370 people are dead, but no-one from this country", which can be interpreted as, "370 not-one-of-us-es have snuffed it, too bad for them, here at home we are all alive na-na-nana-naa!!" In short, instead of watching things which would have otherwise made me lose my legendary good humour, there were a few computers in the occupational therapy room on which I started to familiarise myself with the world of cybernetics. And in this way, I had already added this small string to my rather meagre professional bow.

Turning Point

9. Choosing reintegration: heigh ho, heigh ho, it's off to work we go…

Once I had made my decision, the reality remained that I lived at 70 kilometres (approximately 45 miles) from Brussels, that I still didn't have a car and knew no-one there. If they hired me, I was going to have to find accommodation with wheelchair access, that was both near my place of work and not too expensive. And what if the school had no wheelchair access? And what about the looks from kids, teachers, parents, would I be able to put up with them? In short, it all seemed about as feasible to me as adjusting the suspender belt on a hippopotamus. And so of course, I accepted. Once again, it was my strategy of moving ahead with everything. Wasn't this leap into the unknown a bit dangerous? No doubt yes, and what of it?

I didn't really want to make conversation with my uncle in the car on the way to Brussels, I watched the countryside pass by without seeing it, I was thinking of my imminent meeting: 'they' were going to read my CV which I had typed on a typewriter a couple of days earlier, and I hadn't even cheated on it. What were they going to think of me? Surely I looked too straight with my shiny shoes and my stripey shirt? What would they ask me? I was going to blush, stammer? Suffice to say, I was about as serene as a goldfish who's been taken out of his bowl for the last ten minutes!

We had arrived. The buildings were impressive, a mixture of stone and brick with numerous grand windows

Turning Point

spread over four or five floors which made you spare a sympathetic thought for the poor glaziers. As you pushed open the impressive wooden entrance, the vaulted ceilings gave you the impression of entering into a church. This sentiment was perhaps less surprising when you knew that the establishment was run by Jesuit priests.

"It's on the left along the middle of the corridor, there's a sign marked 'Management' on the door", said the smiling lady who acted as the concierge. The school was comprised of a primary section on the ground floor and a secondary section upstairs. It was the primary school which needed my services. Knock knock sounded my trembling fingers on the finely carved wooden door that would have made Mr Ikea weep with suppressed envy, I had obviously not noticed the bell on my right above which a green button suddenly lit up the word "Enter". Action! On my left, just inside the entrance, there was a huge table covered in paper and files which partly hid the body of a man with greying hair whose only visible features were his severe face and glasses on the end of his nose. A little further on, also on the left, sitting behind a desk scarcely less encumbered with paper, was the Headmistress, whose task it was to judge whether or not I merited a chance.

She rose to greet me her hand extended. She was between 40 and 50 years old and wore a severe suit, a severe hairstyle and a severe blue-eyed gaze. She had something I didn't: natural authority which translates as having no difficulty in being obeyed. Then came the shaking of finger bones, "my name is Viviane F" – Hello, pleased to meet you, I replied with that innate sense of unexpected repartee so characteristic of me. "May I introduce you to M.T. who stops me from drowning under all this paperwork", another game of handshakes. Now that he was standing

9. Choosing reintegration

in front of me and I could return his piercing gaze with its little glimpse of cunning, I guessed that M. T. was no ordinary pen-pusher. He went and dived back into his sea of papers while Mrs F. sat back down at her desk. She took hold of my CV which she read without saying anything. During the few minutes it took for her to run over these sparse lines, I had time to glance outside, out the large window with its view over one of the playgrounds which was silent and empty it being August. A school without pupils resembles a puppet without the hand that brings it alive, it is inert, apathetic, purposeless. .

"You see, she said resting her eyes on me, we have more than 500 pupils at the primary school, as well as a significantly sized academic team, and corresponding document management for all of that which is becoming problematic. Therefore, in addition to the normal administrative tasks that M. T. will be able to explain to you, you will have to try out different software programmes and chose the best to computerise the management of the primary school. Do you feel up to the task?" "Of couurrse – I replied surprising even myself with the assurance in my voice – at the hospital, I had the opportunity to try out many different programmes on lots of different computers. It should be fine".

Obviously, I had no idea whether or not I would be capable of doing the job, but what could I do other than reply in the affirmative? And I think she knew that...

"I will take a copy of your CV. I have another two candidates to see and then we will call you before the end of the month to inform you of our decision. Thank you for coming", she added as she stood up and extended her hand to me, signaling to me that the interview was over.

Turning Point

M. T. diligently came to open the door for me, gratifying me with a "Until the next time perhaps!" while shaking my paw.

See you soon, yeah, perhaps or perhaps not. Generally speaking, "we will call you back" is not the best sign to hear. Moreover, I had not uttered more than five sentences, how could she judge my capabilities merely after a few minutes' interview? However, despite this, I had a good feeling about it, but it's true that at twenty two years old if you have a good feeling about things, it's first and foremost because you can't imagine for a split-second that your 'antennae' could be off.

I'd now been waiting for the telephone call for two weeks, I was simply trying not to think about it too much, I say "I was trying".... I had not had any other job offers in the meantime, so was setting a lot of store on this one, it was the school in Brussels or twiddling my thumbs at Mum's.

In those days the mobile phone only existed in science-fiction films and the telephone apparatus itself was intimately acquainted with the notion of immobility, its cord being attached to the wall. As time passed, I realised I wasn't managing to move very far away from Graham Bell's invention. Each time it rang, it sparked a hope, extinguished immediately by a familiar voice at the other end of the line, until the end of August when I finally heard: "Mr Veulliet? Hello, M. T. from St Michel College here, if you are still okay, you can start with us once the first rush of school in September is over, on 1st October at 8.30am, when we'll have more time to show you your work. Is that okay?" Light, I felt light, airy even "Thank you M. T., thank you very much. Sounds perfect to me, it's

9. Choosing reintegration

a date for 1st October at 8.30am then, uh, have a good... uh... return to classes".

When my mother returned from shopping, she had not even had time to put her bags down before I announced the good news to her. "1st October you say, well, that leaves us less than a month to find you accommodation near to the school and not too expensive either, have you any idea?!" You can always count on your mother to bring you back down to earth...

Turning Point

10: Reintegration means choices: a room with a view

One lead, that's all I had: when I had spoken to the social worker at the CTR about the possibility of working at the school, he'd informed me of the existence of a Catholic hostel near the school which welcomed disabled people for not very much money. To say I was crazy about the idea of finding myself at the heart of this community would obviously be more than an exaggeration, so before accepting this option, I had quickly had a look at the small ads in attempt to find a flat in the neighbourhood. Having made a few calls to landlords, I very quickly learned that I had about as much chance of finding an apartment available at such short notice as I had of finding a nun at a Marilyn Manson concert. As for the rents that were being suggested, I almost wanted to laugh when I heard the amounts.

So I headed for the Catholic hostel one rainy morning in September for an appointment with the director. We visited the residence: the accommodation building was situated on a grand avenue in Brussels in an area which breathed the calm of the old bourgeoisie. It was one of those places where you imagine that the end of the month is not the most preoccupying problem for the local populace, and at the same time, there are no obvious displays of wealth on show, no going shopping dressed to the nines, no flashiness. If you bump into a bloke getting out of a Jaguar, he'll be the first to wave to you. In short, this little

Turning Point

corner of Brussels was rather chic. The building itself was what you'd call a Brussels style 'mansion', narrow, at least four floors high with an attic, with huge adjoining rooms on the ground floor whose vaulted ceilings, decorated with superb sculpted freezes were so high that they made heating installation experts swoon in ecstasy. There was a finely-worked ramped stairway starting from the corridor and getting lost in the house's summits which led you to a number of bedrooms, exactly how many I had absolutely no idea, on each floor. Everything smelled of old stone and oak wood, it was the kind of habitation so solid it had been able to witness the passage of generations of Brussels's citizens. But in order that it remain standing, it needed more upkeep than a bit of hoovering here and some screw-driving there, as there were corners of tiles missing, doors with wood crying out in sufferance at the pieces that had been torn away, which led me to think that it was wasn't that simple to find the money necessary to repair all of this.

The house was a dignified old lady, she was still going strong but her wrinkles were digging in deeper and deeper.

The back of the house overlooked a garden some ten or so metres long with a lawn separated in two by a paved path, surrounded by rosebushes and trees. At the end of this garden there was another long, flat building where I learned my bedroom was situated. On the right as you entered there were two big washing machines and just opposite in order to access my potential bedroom, I had to climb up a sloping plane with such a steep incline, unless they equipped it with a ski tow of the type they use in Courchevel, I would never be able to reach my pad on my own. This didn't seem to present a problem to the director who informed me with a smile that there would always

10: Reintegration means choices

be someone to help me get up the slope. First bad point: for those who liked to be totally autonomous, we'll come back to that...

Arriving at the top of the ramp thanks to the powerful push of this lady who evidently had experience of the exercise, I opened the door to my future bedroom. It was composed of a small narrow bed on the right which was hidden just behind a two-seater sofa and, on the left, I saw a wardrobe right next to a sink. Second bad point: the room was so narrow it would have given a tinned sardine the blues, narrow to the extent that I wanted to fold in on myself, I had to reverse out into the corridor and do a U-turn before finding my way home!

Once back in the principal building, in the lounge, I made the acquaintance of a few of the residences regular inhabitants: a young boy with Down's Syndrome, a mentally retarded lady in her forties and a man of the same generation with cerebral-motor disability. So for me, who had so not wanted to find myself in a 'disabled ghetto', it didn't bode well!

As you can imagine, the idea of spending my evenings and nights in this place did not fill me with ecstasy, but on the other hand, the rent was very low and the proximity of this house to my future place of work were two weighty arguments. I was at this stage in my reflection when the decisive element in favour of the Catholic hostel materialised in the form of a lady who entered the lounge while we were all still united there. She must have been in her fifties, not very tall but her stature betrayed an inner strength more suited to building cathedrals than serving mass for Mr Pastor. In effect, a cross pinned to her jacket identified her as being a religious person who introduced

Turning Point

herself by the name of Sister Agnès. I learned later on that she was originally from the Ardennes region. A single exchange of looks and I realised immediately that she and I would get on just fine. Her short grey hair framed a face, no, rather, a 'mug': a square jaw and a frank look, a knowing mixture of hardness and softness. Even if she hadn't said she was responsible for the hostel, I would have guessed as much, and the fact that she limped because of weak ankles took nothing away from her entirely natural authority. Moreover, following the many conversations we had together late in the evening during the few months I spent at the hostel, I came to realise that for certain women, marrying themselves to God did not mean drying out their hearts in the leaves of the Bible, on the contrary, they used their faith not as a shield but as a bridge to reach out to the other. It was precisely because we weren't in agreement that our exchanges were interesting, it's difference which makes for the real richness, it's others who are going to make you evolve, not change radically, just evolve.

11. Instructions for reintegration: let's get to work!

The children were already in their classrooms when I arrived at the school for my first day of work at the administrative offices. As I entered the director's office she came to greet me with a big smile: "Welcome to our school!" Having shaken my hand, M. T. pointed out a table to me which had not been there at the time of my first visit to the place, at the far end of the office, opposite the big window. "That's your desk". On top of it was an electronic typewriter surrounded and nearly drowned by hundreds of precariously balanced forms. "Your first task will be to file away these forms in the files for each pupil which you'll find in these drawers, then set up a new filing system based on new lists of classes for this academic year" M. T. told me. I will remind you, dear attentive and fascinated readers, that in the beginning I had principally been hired to computerise the school's administration system, yet there were no more computers in the office than sparks of intelligence amongst the participants of Big Brother. "Great, I'm the pen-pusher now!" I said to myself as I shot such a dazzling smile at M. T., it would have made two generations of toothpaste manufacturers happy. I'd been playing silly buggers with the forms for about two hours when the bell for break time rang. In the corridors, I expected to hear the sound of a herd of pupils racing around the courtyard, similar to a troop of African buffalo running from a Savannah fire, a bit like me when

Turning Point

I was in primary school… but not at all, the pupils went outside in rows of two under the supervision of their teacher: the discipline of it, incredible?!

Once the corridors were empty again, the headmistress said to me: "Come along; we're going to have a coffee in the staffroom and I'm going to introduce you to everyone". I had been thinking about this moment all morning, me on four wheels and them standing, we had never seen each other before, they, no doubt, had no experience of mixing with paraplegics, what would be their reaction? Who would be the most ill at ease, me or them? Should I talk to them about my accident? Should I just carry on 'as if'? Nobody could reply to these questions for me and there, in front of the entrance to the staffroom, I still didn't know what attitude to adopt. When I tried to breathe normally I had the impression that a Sumo wrestler was sitting on my ribcage, my hands were so wet they could have made the ink run on the pupils' forms I'd been handling since the morning. And so there we were, Mrs F opened the door and two dozen pairs of eyes fell on me, not in a really surprised way, just curious. Evidently, the boss had given them the lowdown. "I'd like to introduce Yves Veulliet, our new colleague. I suggest that you take it in turns to introduce yourself individually. Coffee, Yves?" "Uh yes please" I replied although obviously, I couldn't have swallowed a drop of anything… "Hello, me I'm Marianne" "Hi, … Roland!" "Welcome Yves, me I'm André". More than twenty teachers introduced themselves to me in this way, my gums hurt from all the smiling. As you can imagine, I was too stirred up to be able to retain a single one of the names. I promised myself that before midday I would take another look at each one of their identity cards to try to avoid making a cock up. A few polite words were exchanged of the kind: "Which region do you come from?

11. Instructions for reintegration

Mons? Oh yesssssssssss, really nice part of the world isn't it!" or: "You'll see: here, I am the nicest of the teachers but him, be careful, he's a lot more sadistic than he looks, you only have to ask his pupils! Hahahaha!!"

Suffice to say, my first contact with the staff hadn't gone too badly, we'd wait and see how the midday meal worked out: obliged to converse with a full mouth, the prospect of exploding mixtures leaving sauce stains on your clothes, all that would be missing would be for them to serve spaghetti bolognaise and the nightmare would be complete!

This meal and all the others which followed, day after day, went well. With the passing of the months, by way of these meals, the breaks during playtime, the drinks after work, little by little the teachers and I helped to bring each other out of our reciprocal shells, they learned to get to know me beyond the wheelchair and me, I did everything I could to make this easy for them.

Allow me to offer you some advice in passing: we are all different, but it's true that some of us are more different than others! If you want the 'other' to look beyond your difference, whatever it is, invite him to do so by putting him at ease with kindness or humour but always with frankness. I hear a whole load of people complaining about being excluded or marginalised in groups for one reason or another. Ladies, gentlemen, the damned of the Earth, don't forget one thing: if you wish for the other person to come towards you, don't make the first step, make much more than that; meeting another is a path that you take together. So why should the other person get landed with the entire path for him alone? I'd go even further, if it's you who is different to the rest, you will have to go most of the path towards the other person on your

Turning Point

own to combat their fears and in this way you'll make a friend or at least an alter ego. If you are not ready to make this effort out of laziness, rebellion or fear, the resulting price to pay will be to find yourself on your own again, navel gazing. Yes, I know it's unfair but it's like that so get moving ye gads!

Having applied this principle, the result was that certain teachers became really at ease with me and my four wheels, inviting me to their place from time to time to spend an evening watching TV, playing board games or just chatting, and this, even when access was not easy: steps at the entrance, narrow doors etc.

Yet a school is not only made up of management, teachers and special needs instructors, it also consists of pupils and parents. As far as the latter were concerned, given that I only met them now and again, I couldn't develop profound relationships with them and so I was unable to influence their way of seeing me. As always in cases like this, when they met me for the first time in the headmistress's office, I often read the surprise on their faces, less often it was pity and fortunately, very rarely, fear.

Another piece of advice in passing (in fact, if my advice gets on your nerves, stop reading this book and throw it away, I got my commission from the moment you bought it!): don't try to be loved by everyone, it's a losing game. You cannot control what others think so just try to be a good person, certain people will appreciate it and others with pass on by, their loss...

So, if relationships with the pupils' parents were rare, it wasn't true for their offspring. I saw them daily and now and again I was in charge of 'study time' after classes which

11. Instructions for reintegration

helped some of them to do their homework if their parents came to pick them up after the last lesson had ended. A kid is powerful and dangerous because they have not yet been corrupted by adult social codes, or not too much anyway. When a kid sees me for the first time, they see that I have normal size legs, that I don't look particularly half-witted and therefore, following their logic, they ask me things like: "Why are you in a wheelchair, are you tired?" "When you want to have a pee, how do you do it?" "That must be great to be sitting down all the time, you jammy geezer!" "It's funny your chair, can you lend it to me?". They are a lethal weapon because they force you to look at yourself without deception, as others see you and not as you wish to be seen. It's surprising, it's destabilising, it's trying, but by goodness, it is more invigorating than diving naked into a Norwegian fjord in the height of winter!

As far as work was concerned, filing forms, typing letters and answering the telephone made up the major part of my work. I felt more and more at ease, and all this in a rather pleasant environment. I really liked the headmistress, Mrs F. Between her at the school and Sister Agnès at the Catholic hostel, I had some formidable allies!

A few months after my arrival, they finally installed the PC I would use to computerise the whole caboodle. I was finally going to be able to test numerous applications and choose the best one for the job with respect to how the school functioned. And so, during the months which followed, I spent most of my time in front of the screen testing the functionality of such or such software programme, and afterwards, in demonstrating it to the headmistress and M. T. The latter, allergic to change in general and to IT in particular, took a perverse pleasure in asking me to produce a whole series of documents and

Turning Point

lists with different criteria for him although he couldn't have cared a less about them, his sole objective was to throw a spanner in the system and on my side, of course, I used my grey matter and put the PC's circuits in overdrive in order to get the data, it was a kind of game between us.

Even if we were very different people; as well as the few decades in age which separated us, he was from a middle class background and very, but I mean VERY Catholic, whilst I'm from a working class background and a bit of an anticlerical, slowly over time, we nevertheless developed a sort of complicity based on our shared mocking, rather acerbic sense of humour.

So, if we were to do a quick assessment after six months in Brussels: concerning the job, I was coping well. I had integrated really well with the teachers, pupils and parents, my major sticking point concerned my accommodation. Despite my excellent relationship with the staff at the hostel and with Sister Agnès in particular, living in a place only partially accessible and where, I had to admit, there weren't many opportunities to slap my thighs with laughter, the desire to take off and make my own modest nest in four new walls gnawed away at me more and more. But to do that, I had to be mobile, to be able to get about within a radius greater than the one my little muscly arms could cope with. As underground systems and buses were not accessible, there was only one solution: a car.

My two-door Opel Kadett was metallic grey with fine red lines down the sides of the doors. It was my key to horizons wider than the one or two kilometres between the school and the Catholic hostel. At the end of each working day, I pored over the newspaper small ads and then set off in my iron horse, going back and forth through the streets

11. Instructions for reintegration

of Brussels and the neighbouring suburbs in search of a new home.

Yet despite all my efforts, the weeks passed with the conundrum of finding an accessible flat that was not too expensive still unsolved. I had of course asked the teachers to keep their eyes open in case they came across that rare pearl and in the end, one of them, Luc heard about a couple of his friends who were putting a small studio up for rent on the ground floor of a modern building in a neighbouring suburb of Brussels. The same evening, Luc introduced me to his friends the owners and we visited the place together. There was neither a step at the entrance to the building nor the flat. The flat consisted of a small hallway, a bathroom/toilet on the left as you entered, then a single L-shaped room with a corner kitchen composed of a hot plate, an oven and a fridge. Having rapidly sized up the available space, I imagined being able to install a bed, a small sofa, a table and a desk. This was more than fine for my needs. In addition, what really seduced me was an entire side of wall made of a big panel of glass which looked out on to the back of the building where a whole lot of greenery had been laid out with numerous paths made of little square slabs of concrete snaking between it. I imagined seeing all that in the middle of the day with the light flooding the studio's main room, yeah, I already saw myself there! So the moment came to raise the thorny question of the cost of service charges for the building and the rent. Thinking about it again today, I believe that my evident joy at the studio (which I never even thought of hiding) and the fact that Luc, the teacher who was with me, was friends with the owners, resulted in them proposing a sum no doubt inferior to that which they'd have offered to an ordinary bloke. With the blissful smile of a lottery winner, I accepted their conditions and that smile did not

Turning Point

leave my face all the while I took Luc home and returned to the hostel. It was only when I ran into Sister Agnès that same evening and announced my imminent departure to her that a veil passed over my zygomatics.

Given that I was the first tenant of this brand new studio, I was able to move in quickly. It was a tradition at the school that the teachers helped each other out with their respective flat moves and so naturally, they all offered to help me move into my new home. But in fact, is it as 'natural' as all that to help each other? Look around you and decide for yourself...

I am about as bothered about harmonising the style of furniture that decorates the place where I live as the mood of a Masaï warrior is influenced by the convulsions of the CAC 40 futures market during hunting season. In one afternoon, I dug up a bed, a wardrobe, a few pieces of furniture with drawers and a whole heap of things absolutely indispensable to modern and masterful man, such as a microwave for reheating ready mademeals and a tin opener for choucroute and cassoulet. The teachers moved all this in in no time at all. Scarcely three days after signing the tenancy agreement, I spent my first night in my new home. The first night was not great as a few hours before we had celebrated my departure from the hostel with a few of the other boarders, instructors and Sister Agnès. She and I knew that our paths had crossed once but that thereafter there was not much chance we'd meet again. It's the rarity of a relationship that sometimes gives it its value. We did not promise each other we would write or that I would return to the neighbourhood, it's not a good idea to tarnish something beautiful by promising lies.

11. Instructions for reintegration

Here I have a confession to make: by way of thank you to the seven teachers who helped me move, who hung things on the walls and moved the furniture into the studio, I had thought of inviting them round one evening to celebrate, and I only ever got as far as thinking about it... I dislike resembling the kind of person I usually scorn.

Turning Point

12. Reintegration continues in a straight line: the theory of perpetual movement

The weeks passed, the months passed and then the first three years, all purring along, a job I managed well, where the atmosphere was good and on the personal front, no major problems. My wheelchair and I were a couple, a marriage of reason. There you have it, purring along nicely, that's okay for cats but not for me!

Do you remember what I wrote earlier in a style to make even Victor Hugo jealous ? My strategy is: "onwards and upwards, only straight ahead", my life seemed to be slowing down and what frightened me was that I was starting to like it that way. Yet, what had made my existence take a different, rather more interesting turn, despite you know what, was the fact that I had impressed regular movement on it. In other words, although I was always sitting on it, I had given myself regular kicks up the bum and I knew that if I were to stop, I would pay for it sooner or later. And what does a young swinging cat of 25 do when he has a steady job and has decided to join his life to a woman he met a few years before?

Yes I know, I could have mentioned this crucial episode in my existence earlier and I am therefore going to do so now, in two lines: I had met C at the end of 1989 and we had been going out together since 1990. Don't expect me to give you more details than that, to commit this side of

Turning Point

my life to paper seems to me as shameless as lifting up the dress of a young lady who hasn't been introduced to me. As you will read further on, this union has produced two children who have become the pillars on which my current life stands. To describe the relationship that I've had with my children in our family setting from birth until today could constitute the subject of a whole book, one perhaps I'll never write.

Serious people call it starting a family; me, I'd say rather that there comes a time when, almost despite ourselves, we all want to play at mummies and daddies because we see other people do it or because we are told to do it or because if we don't do it, we are scared to be the black sheep, and I have to admit that in my case, there existed an additional, extraordinarily powerful motivation: I wanted to prove to myself and to others that I could do this as well. The wrong reason, you'll no doubt be thinking, but those who are reading this who have taken the same decision to have children, should look deep within yourselves: are you sure that what motivated you was just the deafening call of wanting to be a parent? Well, let's see.

But, playing mummies and daddies in a studio like the one I rented which didn't even have a separate, small single bedroom, was about as realistic as trying to teach a legless cripple to do entrechats. We quickly realised that flats and houses in the Brussels area which were in our budget, were so spacious and luxurious they would have depressed a cockroach! And even if we distanced ourselves further from our respective workplaces, the price of accommodation were still too high for our modest budget. The conclusion was obvious: we'd only ever get to buy a house with four walls, a lawn and a dog to run around on it if we robbed a bank or alternatively, I had to find another

12. Reintegration continues in a straight line

part-time job so as to go along to the bank with enough guarantees in hand for the gentleman banker to lend us what we were missing, and all that with a smile. Given that our style was not very Bonnie and Clyde, all that was left for me to do was find a second job.

Do you know much about judo? The Japanese martial art which exists only on condition that there are two of you on the tatami mat, it's only the movements of the other that make it possible for you to put your technique in practice and destabilise your opponent. I'm speaking here of academic judo, not those sporting jousts where you see two gazelles or two bears, depending on the category, trying, often in vain, to avoid the swipes or shoulder movements of the adversary by adopting the position of constipated sumo wrestlers! Dare I compare life to this noble art? It is impossible to advance in life unless others are there to propose different paths to you, up to you to take them or not and, in turn, for you to show the way to others. It's in this way that I heard about IBM: the social worker at the rehabilitation centre had asked me to help her persuade patients that as a paraplegic, it was still feasible to work, not easy but feasible. And so that day after our discussion with them, I spoke to her about my desire to find a second job and that's when she advised me to send my CV to IBM for a job as an administrative assistant (a politically correct term for 'secretary'). She knew a paraplegic employee who had worked there for a number of years. So that's what I did.

A few months later, at the beginning of November 1991, I received a letter inviting me to come along to their offices in order to take aptitude and language tests. Four or five hours in an office at the top of a tower in the centre of

Turning Point

Brussels sitting mental agility tests, taking dictations in English and Dutch, composing letters etc.

It was only when you had passed these tests that you could round off this cerebral marathon with an interview which would evaluate your motivation, aptitudes, etc, conducted by a recruiter.

The coffee I was drinking while waiting for the results had no doubt been excellent at the moment of preparation, approximately three weeks earlier, but I was too stressed to really take offence. It's only when the female recruiter invited me to step into her office for the interview that I realised that I had passed the first part. At the end of the interview, she said to me with a smile: "Thank you for your interest in our company, if an opportunity arises we will definitely call you".

"We'll call you" is the kind of phrase that can bring you down for the rest of the day, a bit like when you say to a woman whose bust is starting to suffer the devastating torments of gravity: "But stop going on Germaine, you *still* look great!" Therefore, I was not very hopeful as I left the IBM building, just wanted to put on my Iron Maiden cassette, at full blast in the car, to flush out my brain.

My visit to IBM's office tower had taken place just over a month ago and I have to admit that my faith in my chances of getting a part-time job with them had somewhat evaporated...always my proverbial impatience... The Christmas holidays were approaching, that blessed period of the year when well-intentioned grandmothers buy yellow and blue diamond patterned pullovers for their grandsons when they were expecting to receive the latest model in the ROBOT-X series with integrated laser or

12. The theory of perpetual movement

when depressed people become depressive and go to buy disposable tissues in boxes of 100. It was at this period then that I found a letter in my postbox, a letter on headed paper from you-know-where, proposing a meeting for a hiring interview with the head of a department who was looking for a part-time administrator in their training centre at La Hulpe, near Brussels. I'll admit that as a Christmas present, it couldn't have been better!

From the road, the only thing indicating that you were at the entrance to the IBM training centre was a flag with the company logo as well as a sign "International Education Centre". You followed a long road lined on each side with trees as far as the eye could see for some few hundred metres before seeing the actual buildings which were spread out over a large area in lots of separate wings. Most of them were no higher than three or four floors, which meant that they were perfectly integrated with the surrounding greenery. In terms of quality of working environment, unless you were a lover of gas leaks and dusty concrete, it was difficult to find anything to fault!

The centre's main activity was to welcome employees and clients from all over the world who came to follow classes in subjects as diverse as IT, management, finance etc.

My future boss, Georges, was of the "we need to get this moving" type, his dynamism was abundant in each of his gestures; 50 years of age, he was short with pepper and salt hair and a stainless steel smile which gave away his long experience in sales. Although his mother tongue was Flemish, his French was perfect, barely twenty minutes of conversation with him was enough to understand that his lively eyes and his ability to adapt his way of being to the person in front of him, all perfectly naturally, must

Turning Point

have made him a devastatingly effective salesman. I later learned that I hadn't been mistaken.

At the end of our meeting, he showed me our offices on the ground floor which comprised two big rooms linked by a door , on the right of which there was an immense window covering the entire length of the two areas, looking out on a large, elegantly paved space surrounded by lawn. The furniture consisted of numerous tables with one or two PCs on each of them, whilst the walls on the left hand side and at the back were hidden by cupboards. I was going to be the secretary for a department providing technical support and marketing for a whole series of IT applications for the whole of Europe. I would have six new colleagues, each one responsible for a specific software application. George presented me to them one by one. Strangely, I was less apprehensive than a few years earlier when I'd been introduced to the teachers at the school, precisely because, perhaps, it was not the first time. Then I met Anne-Marie, the lady I was going to replace, who was soon to be the centre director's new secretary.

When you start a new job in a new environment, your first impressions remain forever engrained for the rest of your career and in that respect, I was very lucky to take over Anne-Marie's position. Her meticulousness, her sense of organisation, her receptiveness to me during the first weeks when I came into her office, which was separated from mine by a mere ten or so metres, about three thousand times a day, each time with a different question, made me understand that I was in the kind of company where being approximate or saying "we'll see" were about as badly tolerated as Denzel Washington at an annual Ku-Klux-Klan barbecue.

12. Reintegration continues in a straight line

Good, okay, from then on it was the school in Brussels in the morning and IBM at La Hulpe in the afternoon, with just enough time at midday to drive between the two. As an aside: how do you eat a sandwich whilst driving when you also have to use your hands to hold the wheel, accelerate and brake? Two arms... Mother Nature, couldn't you have given us three or four for Christ's sake!

Turning Point

13. A turning point in reintegration: one man, two worlds

The two worlds of education and business I mixed in every day had little in common, and this, by the way, this sort of daily intellectual gymnastics was what I really liked. After a few years at this rhythm, in 2000 I decided to give in my notice at the school for three reasons: the first was that I realised I wanted to spend a little more time watching my son, born in 1997, growing up, before, that was, I received an invitation announcing his impending marriage, I should spend a bit more time at home and less on the road. The second reason related to my function at IBM at the time: having been a secretary for two years, I had been put in charge of the IT service for the 'public affairs' department which was working closely with European institutions. It was clear to me that when my esteemed managers had to wait half a day longer from me to be provided with the information they'd requested, this didn't contribute to putting a radiant smile on their faces which were already lit up by the sun setting over La Hulpe. And the last reason was the retirement of both the headmistress of the school, Mrs. F. and M. T.; I quite quickly worked out that the new headmistress and I were not exactly cut from the same cloth and that it was highly improbable we were going to set up a successful textiles factory together. This state of affairs was not unfortunately made any easier by the warm presence of Micheline, whom Mrs. F. had hired some time earlier to take care of the accounts, and with whom I shared an office at the school. Micheline was

Turning Point

the only person I knew in the world with whom it was absolutely impossible to argue. My farewell drinks were less emotional than I had imagined, we promised each other, a few of the teaching staff and me, that we'd stay in contact, that we wouldn't leave each other 'like that' after being together almost every day for more than ten years... but nothing is immune to time, absolutely nothing.

So there I was entirely dedicated to my job as 'information officer' at IBM, which pleased my superiors (who I mentioned earlier) no end and who were able, thanks to my now working full time and to the development of high speed Internet, to access everything they needed when and where they wanted.

That was at the end of 2000, one year before the birth of my second child, a daughter. IBM had left its offices near Mother Nature in La Hulpe as well as the tall office tower in the centre of Brussels in which I had taken my tests and hiring interviews, in order to group together the majority of its personnel in the suburbs of Brussels, in a brand new modern building complex surrounded by a type of nature reserve where you'd guess that any blade of grass not grown with the help of man would be considered a renegade of the human order, a Che Guevara of lawns.

There is a harmless joke that goes around at IBM: what do the three letters I.B.M. stand for? Reply: "I've Been Moved". It's true that the world of information technology evolves so quickly that the way in which you do your job will no doubt be completelyoutmoded in the eight months that follow and if you are not particularly flexible in your approach to accept these incessant changes, a serious nervous breakdown could be heading your way! My job at that time was no exception and I could feel that profound

13. A turning point in reintegration

changes at the start of the 21st century in terms of information access and the speed with which information was produced were going to have short term consequences for my job (note: I'm aware that this last phrase could have been written by a spotty, 17 year old student in his end of year dissertation, I am dying of shame but I am not brave enough to change it). As a consequence, I began to look for another role in the company. Luckily for me, I quite quickly obtained a meeting with the head of a team of consultants who were looking for someone to identify new business opportunities at a European level, to assure the coordination between internal consultants and external partners, and ensure that the proposal submitted to the client complied with terms and conditions.

German, Italian, French, Canadian, Spanish, English, American... these were some of the nationalities of people I had worked with since joining IBM. If you want to dust the cobwebs off those prejudices and stereotypes which make us all shortsighted about others, this experience is irreplaceable. If a South African says to you "I hear you", that does not mean that he agrees with you, it just means he has understood what you are saying to him. If a French person says to you "Yes but...", this obviously means that he agrees with you but that he has an objection, but if a Chinese person says the same thing to you, it means "No". It's true that in a professional setting this can play tricks on you (and I know what I'm talking about!) but after years of collaborating like this, you end up being able to see things through the other person's eyes. You should never miss a chance to become a little less stupid.

Well, for a change, the new team I'd just joined consisted only of Belgians with one or two exceptions. I only stayed two years in this department, from 2003 to 2005. The

Turning Point

extraordinarily repetitive and monotonous type of work left about as much room for creativity and imagination as a porno film keeps secret the female anatomy. As a consequence, I regularly consulted the internal website advertising new available jobs. And it was on this site one day in March 2005 that to my great astonishment, I saw the advertisement for the European 'Workforce Diversity' team who were looking for a new team member responsible for managing existing programmes and creating new ones in order to encourage the integration of guess who? Of... of...yes, of handicapped people within the company! If I could have, I would have leapt out of my chair! That same evening I updated my CV on which I mentioned my various functions in-house as well as an exhaustive list of all the internal training courses I'd followed every year since entering the company and sent it by email to the contact person. Obviously, I was not the only person being considered for the role, Edith, the said point of contact, confirmed to me at our first meeting. After an initial shortlist selected from our CVs, there were still three of us in the running. But as I didn't know the names of the other two candidates, it was unfortunately impossible to put a bomb under the hood of their car or to make them fall down the stairs; therefore, I had to rely solely on my kills, not only to convince Edith, but also the 'Team Leader', an American, that I was the Big, the Handsome, the Unique, the Majestic Yves she'd been waiting for, unbeknown to her, like the Messiah himself!

To have my first telephone conversation with her, I shut myself away in one of the most discrete, small offices. I knew that this moment would determine whether I would join the 'diversity' team or continue in my current job. At the end of our Graham Bell exchange, my impression was that it had gone quite well. I had only to wait a few days for

13. A turning point in reintegration

Edith to call me back to tell me whether I was the Chosen One, or not....

Two days later, Edith's extension number appeared on my fixed line. Deep breath: "Hi Edith – Hi Yves, all well with you? – Yes, not bad thanks and you? – Fine yes, thank you". During this conversation whose originality will have escaped no-one, my heart had a very strong desire to come up for air and had begun its ascending path to my mouth. "We'd like you to join the team for the month of June, that should leave you enough time to ensure the handover in your current job, shouldn't it?"

It's now been more than four years since I've worked with Edith and what I love about her and means that we work well together is that she has taken her motto from the following geometric principle: the straight line is the shortest distance between two points. As a consequence, she only burdens herself with the minimum social requirements and then passes the main message over to you without beating about the bush and without any unexpected twists, and whether it be positive or negative, you know what you are getting for your money.

When my Eustachian tubes heard the sentence confirming my integration in the ;diversity; team, my lungs understood that air could once again circulate in them and my heart finally forgot its desire to run away, which allowed me to reply: "That leaves me two months to organise my departure and we can start to meet up regularly so that you can get me up to speed before I officially start the job" – perfect, speak to you soon! – Click!

I had already informed my close colleagues of my desire to leave and had already identified the person in the

Turning Point

team who could take over my role. They were therefore not surprised about my imminent departure and took it rather well. Please allow me once again, dear You who are currently reading this magnificent book at your place of work while kidding your boss that it's the company annual report you're holding in your hands, to pass on a tip: be honest, don't hide your desire for change behind your desire to maintain harmony and therefore keep it from your boss (this of course is much easier to achieve within an organisation that favours a policy of internal mobility across its different sectors of activity). But be constructive in your communication, better to say: "I don't feel comfortable in my current job, I get the impression that I'm not fulfilling this role in a way that the team has the right to expect. If it's okay with you, I am happy to help you find someone who'll be better in the role than me", rather than: "I'm going round and round in circles here and I want to tell it to you straight, as soon as I find something that suits me better, it's ciao, bye bye!" This kind of sentence, although having the merit of being rough and ready in its sincerity, is more likely to earn you the right to a one way ticket to the fascinating world of unemployment than a ticket to professional Nirvana!

14. The gentle slope of reintegration: a mobile job with reduced mobility

As I already said, Edith is one of those "1+1=2 and not 1.9 or 2.1" managers and from our very first meeting when most people would have taken a much more convoluted path to ask me this question, it seemed the most natural thing in the world when she stated: "Your role involves a lot of travel by plane and train all around Europe. Will the fact that you get around in a wheelchair present a problem or not?" What's great about frank people is that they give you the impression your progressing on solid ground, and what's more, they push you to look yourself squarely in the eye (an exercise which requires either a good mirror or incredible ocular flexibility, I admit!) So, to be clear, I asked myself the following question: "As far as international train and airplane accessibility are concerned, there aren't any real problems, on the other hand, I too have the same problems as everyone else: with regard to family, two not-very-old children and a wife who works exclusively in the evenings, more than once a week, so how are you going to juggle all that smarty pants?" (as you will observe, I know myself well, which simplifies life because we have no choice but to live together from our first howl to our last breath).

It was almost quite reassuring to remark that for once, the predominant problem did not lie with my wheelchair, but was a question of work/life balance which could have concerned anybody, whether valid or not. But reassuring or not, the problem was still there. And because we lived

Turning Point

in the middle of the country, finding a babysitter who would be sufficiently autonomous and flexible to come at irregular hours and on irregular days seemed about as easy as finding an electric iron in an Palaeolithic tomb!

The only solution was to take each trip as it came. I must have caused a fair number of cases of stress-related weight gain among the travel agency employees taking care of my ticket reservations. To be able to find train or plane times which allowed for me to meet clients or partners in their country whilst spending enough time there to progress with our work and also leaving enough time for me to return home to play Dad without being late, while Mum in turn, left for work to also bring home the bacon, I must have asked these poor travel experts to plan schedules for me that would make the hardest brainteasers seem like child's play for the mentally retarded!

Despite frantically racing through the labyrinth of suitcases at airports on my four wheels, despite my chronically constipated smile when my taxi once again found itself held up in a traffic jam in some town centre or other when I knew that my plane was taking off in an hour, despite the Jamaican tourist just in front of me at hotel reception who was arguing for twenty minutes about paying for a packet of minibar peanuts which she denied having ingurgitated, despite computer failure at thingy airport which would delay all takeoffs for ten hours, and despite half a billion other supplementary reasons which made these trips recurring causes of stomach ulcer, yes, I liked it, I liked seeing new places, meeting new people, breathing new odours, seeing other skies, learning how to say "thank you" in Hungarian or "hello" in Finnish, and I also liked it because once again my wheelchair was no longer an insurmountable obstacle...

15. A conclusion and two necessities: accessibility and…

So there you have it, I've now been in the job for four years, our current team is spread over Belgium, France, England, Germany, Romania and Austria, we don't see each other much but we speak to each other a lot. The nature of the job is constantly evolving, there are changes of programme, strategies are modified, organisations adapt and my colleagues and I do everything we can to go with the flow, with diversity, not only in our work but also on a personal level.

What makes me believe that, up until now, I have won my bet to reintegrate with society, is not the travel, is not the suits and ties, is not my alcoholic Texan cowboy accent when I speak English, is not the air of inspired storyteller I take on when I make a presentation in front of an audience. No, what I am bloody proud of having achieved is that when the majority of people who know me, be they Pakistani military personnel, a nun from the Ardennes, a German businessman or a Czech university professor get sight of me, what they see is not a guy in a wheelchair but Yves who happens to *use* a wheelchair.

I'm winning against no-one, I don't beat anybody, it's a victory over myself and only I know the prize. The answers to your problems, whatever they are, are to be found inside you, absolutely nowhere else, but don't make the mistake of looking for them on your own. It's all the

Turning Point

people I have met as recounted in this book and of course many others who have made me less blind, a little more open to the world around me.

Don't close yourself to others, or if you do, get ready for a much severer handicap for the rest of your life than a wheelchair.

Here's where I've decided to stop telling my story which I hope, will help those who find themselves in a difficult situation to see the light, however faint it may be, in the middle of their dark night. I also spare a thought for those close to and around them: families, friends, health professionals, etc..., I believe that they might also be able to find elements amongst these lines which will help them to even better supervise, help and support the least lucky amongst us.

I'm now 44. My journey from 12th July 1987 to the present day could have been a lot easier, and that unfortunately is still true today, if only two states of affairs, to help us start out on this new life, were improved. The first necessity is to make our immediate environment accessible. The notion of handicap is intimately linked to the notion of restriction in the use of resources offered to one and all.

Yet, it would only take real awareness, and with it real willingness, and a bit of money, for this obstacle to become a relic of the past. The following couple of 'open letters' explain how and why this can be achieved.

As for the second, more intimate necessity, which is more susceptible to extremely powerful cultural taboos, I will leave you to find out what it is over the next few pages...

First necessity:
Access for people with disabilities: no.
Access for everybody: yes!

To You, The Reader,

I know that like me you go to the cinema, the theatre, for a drink, or even, let's be crazy!, to the post office or the town hall. If you have to climb up three steps or a narrow doorway to access a building, you have no difficulty but for me and the millions of people like me, it causes a whole load of frustration, imposed inequalities and stupid material limitations which often have a naughty habit of wiping the beatific smile from my face, time and time again!

Whether you are involved in public office, a tradesman or a simple man in the street, the following few lines are addressed to you.

To The Lawmakers,

Today, the prevailing legislative arsenal makes provision for existing public buildings to be made accessible to handicapped people as quickly as possible and for all new buildings to be accessible by default and this is all to the good.

However, there are laws and there is real life. Dear political decision makers, in order for you to take stock of the reality experienced by a certain section of the population that

Turning Point

elected you, I can only heartily encourage you to ensconce your majestic backsides in the soft hollow of a wheelchair for a few hours or to totally obscure your eyes and get on a bus, train or underground system to take you to the post office, the town hall or to the ministry of some such or other and I don't doubt for a minute that you will taste with unfeigned pleasure the delights of pavements that are too high, unmarked obstacles, entrances with steps but no ramp, ticket offices and reception desks that are too high and prevent the smiling employee from lighting up at the joyful sight of the person who is hidden 50 cm lower down in a wheelchair.

Once this priceless, nightmarish experience is over, you will leave your wheelchair or your opaque glasses and return your posterior to the fresh land breeze, your eyes to the warm light of a comforting sun, but I know that you will never forget that certain of your citizens are not that lucky and as a consequence, you will take action so that public places are REALLY accessible not just for handicapped people but for *everybody*: if a wheelchair can get through, so can a pushchair, a cane and its owner, and even, to round it all off perfectly, an ordinary being who has no need of a chair or a cane.

Act now and believe that come the day of the elections, we, our families and all those close to us will know who to vote for!

Lady and gentleman restaurateurs, cafe owners, bakers, greengrocers, and owners of theatres, museums, cinemas, and other places of debasement or elevation of the human spirit (which are more often than not, one and the same),

First necessity

You run these establishments to make money, a noble endeavour in itself. Let me draw your attention to the following fact: it cannot have escaped your attention that our continent's good old population is ageing and that, as a result, more and more people are faced with diverse and varied physical problems which prevent them from getting to your stunning establishments. This segment of the population represents a not insignificant and continually expanding share of your potential clientele. Whatever type of establishment you run, a simple investment to make it fully accessible would allow you to attract new regulars, be they beer drinkers, theatre goers or furniture buyers.

Not only would you be doing a good social deed but in addition, you would increase your revenues. We often keep our wallets near to our hearts, so why not please both!

Turning Point

Dear All Of You,

You, Madam, bitterly regret that after your ski accident in Courchevel which resulted in you having to spend a few weeks in a wheelchair, you were unable to go to see the latest film starring Brad Pitt, with whom, by the way, you have no doubt you'll have an affair as soon as he's dumped that horrible ugly duckling, Angelina. You, Sir, promised your sweet darling that in less than a week you will have totally repainted the cellar, but that was six months ago. And so, descending the steps to this cherished cellar with a desire to get on with it at last, your ankle gives out and you're in plaster for a fortnight. So that's the end of football matches on TV at your friend's flat because he lives on the third floor without a lift.

And what about you, Ladies and Gentlemen, who have a sister-in-law working at the Department of Housing, a cousin who owns a cinema or a playing field with a cafeteria on it, an architect husband...go on, spread the word, get their attention on matters of accessibility, insist that they respect them and you too can get married to Brad Pitt or enjoy your footballing exploits at your mate's place on the third floor even if, you are temporarily on four wheels.

Accessibility is not a question of disability, it concerns us all!

Go on, pass it on!

Second necessity: don't tell me you haven't thought about it?

The Anglo-Saxons have an expression I really like to describe what everyone is thinking about but nobody is saying: "The elephant in the room". So, since the beginning of this story, there has been a very present 'elephant in the room', I might even go as far as to say it's omnipresent.

What does a man think about every 33 seconds or thereabouts? What's the most used word on the Internet? Why are there songs like "If only we could see up girls' skirts»? Just to remind you, I was a lad of 21 years old at the time of my accident and what obsesses us, we blokes at that age (and long afterwards)? Our social status? Our blossoming career? World hunger? My step sister's phlebitis? ...Babes and babes only, my friend!!

The seasonal fluctuations of a dyed-in-the-wool heterosexual bloke go something like this: spring with its light dresses, summer with its procession of short skirts, autumn with its rustle of silk stockings and winter with its opaque tights. Following my first few months in hospital and my first time in a wheelchair which I've described as forcibly as possible (see earlier chapters), when I realised that from now on there would be a 'before' and an 'after' 12th July 1987, the first question to bang violently at the door of my conscience was: "Could I still be attractive to women?" And its corollary: "If so, how do you make love without moving your legs? And the sensation, would I still

Turning Point

feel something? And the woman, would it turn her on or would she struggle to stifle a yawn?"

These were questions of the utmost importance, but who could I ask? If I have a problem concerning my blood circulation, there's no cultural pressure to prevent me from questioning the doctors about it, but on the subject of slap and tickle, it was another case entirely. The doctors who came to see me in my room during their rounds asked me: "So how's it going today? Ready for your physio? You should be eating a bit more!" No male or female doctor for that matter ever turned up to ask the following questions: "So, still waking up with an erection? And pulling birds in the corridors, that going okay? How many women's heads have you turned today?"

One or two doctors at the rehabilitation centre were able to answer my questions on the quality of erection and ejaculation and on my chances of having children, that's to say from a scientific, technical point of view. But as the saying goes "There's many a slip 'twixt the cup and the lip" (and I leave each of you to your own devices in bringing your own interpretation to the word "lip"...). I tried to gen up on the subject by asking 'old timer' paraplegics about their own experiences and I have to say that the reassuring replies of my more experienced partners in crime concerning the concrete aspects of things, while the doctors tended to concentrate more on the scientific aspects, gave me a bit more confidence in myself regarding my ability to seduce, but only a bit.

As luck would have it, I was single at the time of the crash, which saved me from the painful experience of 'getting back into bed with the Missus': inevitably any comparisons with 'before' would have hurt, it would take to find your

Second necessity

feet again, investigate what was possible, realise your limitations, all that whilst trying to make it seem that everything was fine... pretty unbearable. Few couples can go through that trial without breakages.

When you learn to ride a bike, it's Daddy or Mummy or Uncle Arthur who is there to guide you. When you kiss the boy or girl you've been dreaming about for months for the first time, it's from the latest schmaltzy romantic movie that you've learned how to French kiss like a demon! When you are ready to get horizontal for the first time, it's either with someone who has already clocked up some flying hours, in which case it's 'automatic pilot' or, your partner is as much a beginner as you and it's 'the discovery of a whole new world' for both of you. In these two situations, you take the great leap together.

So now imagine someone who has a medullary injury and is obliged to replay the 'first time' scene with a partner who although full of goodwill, has never before been confronted with this situation. You might have guessed that the outcome is often what you'd call disastrous, catastrophic, devastating, tragic, a "Waterloo, dismal plain!", as Victor Hugo summed it up. A bit like when you house is ravaged by fire in a storm and you realise that your insurance cover ran out a month ago.

However, the same goes for sex as for the rest of your apprenticeship for this new life, little by little, experience after experience, your pleasure returns, and you notice, not without a certain amount of happiness, that you can give pleasure too. But, in God's name, when they teach us to climb kerbs in our chair, there is a physio with us; when we practice putting our wheelchair in the car, there is an occupational therapist with us; when we have to relearn

Turning Point

how to make love, who's there to help? Who guides us? Who educates us? The response is blindingly clear: nobody, Jack shit, nothing, not a chance!

So, at the risk of setting teeth gnashing among the respectable classes or narrow-minded doctors: in the same way that there are nurses, occupational therapists, doctors, physios, social workers and others who are there to help and guide us in our new lives, why not automatically include sexual reeducation as part of the standard programme?

Yes it's trivial, yes it's shocking, yes it's inconvenient, yes it's coarse, yes it's unseemly, yes it's licentious but it's only when this aspect of rehabilitation is yanked from the shadows of stifling prudishness that we'll get human beings who are, without doubt messed up but, ready, truly ready to look the world in the eye and say "I'm here, I count!"

Annex:
How I have made my life bearable

Reading someone's story is only interesting if you can take from it something for yourself, which is why I would like to share with you some of the principles that have helped to direct me through life, in the hope you'll find amongst them something to make your life a little lighter too.

Freedom: only two principles lead to real freedom: free yourself of all attachment to possessions and always look to maintain harmony in your relationships with others. Both are very difficult, and I have yet to manage them.

Happiness: don't chase after that which does not exist. The notion of happiness implies stability and permanence. What a joke! Everything changes, everything is constantly evolving, both good and bad things. Try instead to glean the most for yourself and your loved ones from moments of joy and try to make them last for as long as possible.

Love: it's when you find it that you start to lose it. So do all you can to make it last; to surprise the other, make them laugh, propose things to them, provoke them. Be it ten days, ten years, thirty years, it doesn't matter, it will always end so live your love day in day out.

Hatred: a dangerous and ridiculous waste of time. Your hatred may hurt your enemy, but one thing is sure, it will destroy you.

Turning Point

Death: does thinking about it all the time prevent it from happening? No. So *carpe diem*, make the most of the moment, yesterday no longer exists and tomorrow may never come. Today IS.

Stress: there are things you can control and others you cannot. Act on what you can and put up with the rest. Example: you arrive late and your train has left: this was in your control and it's your fault. Do what you can to avoid it happening again. The train is late and you are going to miss your meeting, this is not in your control, buy a magazine.

Others: use their qualities, their skills, their gifts but above all let them use yours and even propose they take advantage of them. It's only in giving that you receive. Some of these people will become your friends, and one things for sure, an even greater number of them will never be your enemies.

Competition: yes, but only with yourself, you will always find someone who is better looking, richer or more intelligent than you. Push your own limits and don't bother about other people's.

www.ingramcontent.com/pod-product-compliance
Lightning Source LLC
Chambersburg PA
CBHW071156090426
42736CB00012B/2354